a Cordwell

Get Past exam Nerves

summersdale

GET PAST EXAM NERVES

www.summersdale.com

Printed and bound in Great Britain

ISBN: 978-1-84024-725-1

Substantial discounts on bulk quantities of Summersdale books are available to corporations, professional associations and other organisations. For details telephone Summersdale Publishers on (+44-1243-771107), fax (+44-1243-786300) or email (nicky@summersdale.com).

About the author

Lorna Cordwell is a therapist and has a private practice in Harley Street, London. She works with clients on a variety of issues and specialises in relaxation work and hypnosis. Many of her clients want to overcome anxiety and fear in situations such as driving tests and academic exams. She has worked, with positive results, with people who have failed tests several times or who have never felt comfortable about taking exams and are at the stage of believing that they will never pass.

Trained in psychology at the prestigious London School of Economics (University of London) and at the National College of Hypnosis and Psychotherapy, she has worked as a therapist since 1987. She is a member of the United Kingdom Council for Psychotherapy, the British Association of Counsellors and Psychotherapists and the National Register of Hypnotherapists and Psychotherapists.

Lorna has also written *Get Past Driving Test Nerves*.

Contents

Introduction

> 'In the exam my mind went blank. I started to read the question over and over again. It wasn't making sense, and I was struggling to remember anything that I had learned.'

Exam nerves are well known to many of us. Throughout our education, and often in our career, we face challenges in order to pursue our goals or get onto the next rung of the job ladder. These challenges often involve written exams.

We can look upon exam time with trepidation, knowing that it is a time of hard work, anticipation and challenge. But for many of us, the exam itself causes our nerves to increase to such an extent that we can feel debilitated by them. We may know our subject well, we may have listened and learned intently throughout the year and we may have revised carefully, but when exam day arrives we can find ourselves overcome with nerves and do not perform as well as we hoped. Why? Because our nerves stop us thinking straight and we panic.

Is this you? If you are concerned that nerves might affect your exam result, then this book will help you to alleviate them through methods commonly used by psychologists and therapists to promote calm and boost self-confidence.

This book will give you a clear understanding of what nerves are, what their purpose is (yes, they do have a purpose) and how you can remain calm and clear-minded on the day.

When you don't feel nervous, you think clearly, recall what you know easily, take instructions comfortably and plan well. In other words, you feel calm and confident – and when you feel calm and confident you do things well.

This book demonstrates simple methods that will instil calm and confidence on the day so you know you are doing the very best you can. What this book cannot do, however, is show you how to pass an exam without knowing the subject. You still need to revise in order to be able to recall your knowledge comfortably.

The main tools used in this book are relaxation scripts. These scripts use hypnotherapy principles to build feelings of calm and confidence specifically for exam time. We cannot feel relaxed and anxious at the same time. So by promoting relaxation, we lessen anxiety. When we are relaxed, we think clearly and perform well.

You will need to record these scripts or have the help of a willing friend to read them to you on a regular basis.

I suggest you begin by reading this book from cover to cover to understand its contents. Then, start the book again and work through the exercises. If you can, start work on the exercises three to four weeks before taking your exams. This way you will gain maximum benefit from the exercises. However, if this is not possible, then start work when you can. Even if you listen to the scripts once or twice before the exam, they will have a positive effect.

Chapter 1

Understanding the vicious cycle of nerves

The psychological term for nerves is anxiety. Anxiety is a set of feelings that are uncomfortable and unpleasant to experience. Typical symptoms of anxiety can include:

- Heart racing
- Breathlessness
- Shaky limbs
- Feeling weak
- Nausea
- Vomiting

- ✓ Needing to go to the toilet more frequently
- ✓ Confusion
- ✓ Inability to recall thoughts
- ✓ Clammy palms
- ✓ Sweating
- ✓ Feeling scared
- ✓ Thinking everything is going wrong

Not a comfortable list, is it? Some people are more prone to anxiety than others but we all feel it, because anxiety is a natural response to a perceived threat. Note that I say a *perceived* threat. This is important in our understanding of anxiety. What one person sees as a threat, another doesn't.

Remember: anxiety is a natural response to a perceived threat.

Now, this definition gives us a big clue about anxiety. You might be surprised to learn that anxiety has a positive purpose. As part of our make-up as human beings, we have what is known as the 'Fight or Flight' response. This response happens automatically. It is controlled by our subconscious mind. Of our total mind capacity, our subconscious makes up around 90 per cent. The rest, our conscious mind, is the part that controls our thoughts and behaviour. This is not to say that we are out of control – just the opposite, in fact. When we are in subconscious control, we are very much in control.

Our conscious mind reacts to the world around us. It deals with a small amount of information at any one time. Everything else is in our subconscious control. This means that we don't have to consciously think about it.

Let's look at an example of this. Can you ride a bike? If so, you might remember a time when you couldn't. As you were learning, you had to really think about it. Keeping the bike upright, pushing off, that difficult bit of trying to get both feet on the pedals while the bike is wobbling around. Then, gathering some speed, a tricky corner and another wobble, trying to coordinate braking, gear changing, pedalling and turning all at the same time. Difficult, wasn't it?

Now that you can ride a bike, when was the last time you thought about any of that? You simply get on the bike and you ride. You think about where you are going, how you are getting there, and you read the road. How is this possible? Well, your ability to ride the bike is now stored in your subconscious mind, so you can do it without having to consciously think about it.

TIP

Remember: your subconscious stores everything you have ever learned or experienced. This means even if you haven't ridden a bike for many years, you could get onto one and still know how to ride it.

Your subconscious also controls your bodily processes. Your body does not have a mind of its own; it does what you tell it to do. Your subconscious controls your heart rate, your blood pressure, the way you digest your food, your eyelids blinking and, of course, it controls your breathing. You know that you can consciously breathe, but you know that you breathe even when you don't think about doing it.

Because your subconscious controls all of these processes, it then regulates them according to what is happening around you.

So, if you need to run for the bus, your subconscious will:

- ✓ Speed up your heart rate
- ✓ Increase your breathing

- ✓ Send extra oxygenated blood to your muscles
- ✓ Enable you to create that burst of speed necessary to catch the bus.

Once you are on the bus, your subconscious recognises that now you are sitting down, and will allow your body to return to normal.

The main purpose of our subconscious mind is one of keeping us safe – a survival instinct.

What has this got to do with anxiety? The subconscious works a lot faster than your conscious mind. If your subconscious thinks you are under threat, then it will send your body into 'Fight or Flight' mode. This means that it makes you ready to deal with the threat – to either fight or run away. If necessary, you would be able to do this better, stronger and faster than you believed you were capable of. We've all heard stories of people finding themselves in dangerous situations and saying afterwards that they didn't know how they managed to do what they did at the time. 'Something' seemed to take over. Yes, it did: that 'something' was their subconscious mind.

All the symptoms of anxiety on the list above are purposefully created by the subconscious if it perceives you to be in danger. Let's look back through the list:

The 'Fight or Flight' response

The subconscious mind releases adrenaline, and produces the following symptoms:

Heart beating faster/ pains in chest
Our heart starts to pump our blood around our system much faster so that all our vital organs are ready to work faster.

Shortness of breath
Our breathing rate increases so that we can move faster.

Arms and legs feeling weak or shaky/ sweating/ feeling faint
Our body releases a surge of adrenalin, which allows our muscles to work much more effectively.

Stomach churning/ feeling nauseous or vomiting/ going very pale

Blood moves to parts of our body that need it most, our vital organs and our muscles, and moves away from other parts of our body that are in less need of it: our stomach for example, where either the digestive process is put on hold, or we eliminate the contents, making us lighter and able to move even faster.

Unable to focus or concentrate

While all this is going on, our mind is automatically planning escape routes, or defences.

The 'Fight or Flight' response is useful and necessary. It is a normal function. The problem is that the 'Fight or Flight' response has not evolved as we have. For all the sophistication of today's society, this response works in the same way every time we perceive a threat. It is very useful to have if we are ever in real danger, but not useful in other situations.

The key to controlling the 'Fight or Flight' response is to work with our perception of a threat. If you view the exam as a threat then your subconscious mind is triggering the 'Fight or Flight' response. Now, we know that the exam is a unique situation and a lot may depend on the outcome. It is good to have some focus and some adrenaline released, but this needs to be at a comfortable level, allowing you to concentrate and to recall the information that you have retained.

The exercises in this book will help you to change your perception of the exam from one of a threatening situation to one of a challenge you can confidently meet. Your subconscious does not respond to a comfortable challenge by evoking the 'Fight or Flight' mechanism and, as a result, you will be in control and focused throughout your exam.

Imagination plays a big role in anxiety. Often, when we feel anxious we are expecting a negative outcome. Are you nervous about the exam because you are expecting to do badly? If you are telling yourself that something is going to go wrong, what is the evidence for this? If you continue to tell yourself that it will go wrong you are creating a threatening situation in your imagination.

If I tell myself over and over again that I will definitely fall over and hurt myself when I leave the house this morning, I can make myself anxious about leaving the house. I can talk myself into believing that the doorstep is a threat. This can set up a vicious cycle of events: I've now told myself so much that I will fall over if I leave the house that I am probably more likely to trip up when I do. Then, when the worst happens, I have confirmed my anxiety and set up a negative cycle of self-perpetuating thoughts and feelings. If you tell yourself that the exam is something to be feared and worried about, then you begin to believe, setting up the same vicious cycle.

Chapter 2

Introducing our 'storehouse' - the subconscious mind

As discussed in the previous chapter, your subconscious mind is controlling all your bodily processes. It stores everything that you have learned and experienced. All the knowledge you have learned and revised over the past years, months or weeks is contained in your memory, which is part of your subconscious.

When you feel anxious, your subconscious is only accessing what you need in order to deal with the threat. A boxer in the ring does not need to start remembering what's on his supermarket shopping list; he just needs to be aware of the threat from his opponent.

When you are relaxed, your mind will recall stored information much more easily.

By relaxed, I mean the opposite of anxious. We can be calm and relaxed and at the same time alert, focused and active. This relaxed state is called the alpha state. This is what is known as a 'brainwave state', where our conscious and our subconscious minds are working in harmony to achieve the best possible outcome for the situation that we find ourselves in. Athletes and sports professionals refer to this state as being 'in the zone'. It describes a certain brainwave state that is relaxed, calm, focused and alert. You might describe someone who is in this state when they are carrying out their work as 'professional'. In other words, they are doing their job really well. The athlete moves and responds incredibly fast but they are inwardly calm and focused.

How does it feel when you are relaxed? Some of the feelings are described here:

- ✓ Relaxed body
- ✓ Comfortable
- ✓ Calm mind
- ✓ Feeling happy
- ✓ Feeling easy
- ✓ Able to think clearly
- ✓ Feeling confident
- ✓ Breathing easily
- ✓ Being in the moment
- ✓ Focused
- ✓ Creative

This is the state that you will achieve with the help of this book. When you take your exam, you can feel calm and relaxed yet focused and alert. Imagine that now for a moment... it feels good, doesn't it? When you feel this way, all your knowledge will be there, ready to access as and when it is required.

Imagine that your memory is like a library. In this library are many shelves of books on all kinds of different subjects. This library is stored in your subconscious mind. You don't need access to all of it all of the time but you do need to be able to access it when you want to.

Some of the shelves in the library contain the information that you need for your exam. These shelves are now becoming quite well used and full of well-thumbed books. You also have shelves of books about planning and setting out information in a clear way. These shelves are not only used for exams – you turn to them for all kinds of tasks that you regularly carry out. This information, made up of experience and learning, could be used for everything from planning a route home to cooking a meal, getting ready to leave the house in the morning or completing a sudoku puzzle. You have a lot of experience of planning in a logical sequence and therefore the same level of experience in retrieving information in a logical way.

Think about cooking for a moment. If you are cooking spaghetti bolognese, you know the order in which to cook the ingredients. Perhaps you chop the onions and garlic first. You retrieve the information on how to chop onions before you need to think about how you cook spaghetti. When the time comes and you have the spaghetti ready, you remember how to add it to the pan and how long to cook it.

When you are recalling information in your exam, you don't need to remember it all. You just need to remember the first piece of information. This will lead to you recalling the next piece, and then the next...

If you give your mind a direction, it will follow it. So, by deciding which shelf you are going to in the library, you have all the information in front of you. You take down the first title that you need and the rest will follow exactly when you need them. As you write, you will be putting books that you no longer need to look at back on the shelf and opening the next volume.

This will happen easily when you are relaxed, because this is how your subconscious mind works. It brings information into your conscious mind. There is always something in your conscious mind; it is never completely empty. However, it cannot store too much information at once. Your conscious mind can hold about seven pieces of information at a time. People talking about their mind going blank in exams – it's not blank, it is filled with other information. If we feel anxious, those seven pieces might be something like this:

'My mind has gone blank.'
'Oh no, I can't remember anything.'
'This is what I thought would happen.'
'I'm breathing really fast now.'
'Everyone around me is doing better than me.'
'I must remember.'
'I wish I could get out of here.'

This stream of consciousness has originated from one initial thought, and the thinker has now created anxiety for themselves which is leading to the 'Fight or Flight' response. As these seven bits of information change, they might generate even less helpful thoughts:

'Everyone around me is doing better than me.'
'I must remember.'
'I wish I could get out of here.'
'I knew I couldn't do it.'
'I'll never get that job now.'
'I've always known I was a failure.'
'Now everyone will know I am a failure.'

Stop. This train of thought has run into a strongly negative direction, and these thoughts are far away from answering the questions set. You are

nowhere near the correct shelf in the internal library.
What we're aiming for is something closer to the popular song 'Dem Dry Bones':

> The foot bone connected to the leg bone,
> The leg bone connected to the knee bone,
> The knee bone connected to the thigh bone,
> The thigh bone connected to the back bone,
> The back bone connected to the neck bone,
> The neck bone connected to the head bone.

How do we get to this place? By being calm and focused. Then the process becomes something like this:

1. Right, what's this question asking?
2. Let's read it again to check.
3. Yes, that is clear.
4. Now, what information do I need?
5. I think it's connected to the knee bone.
6. The knee bone connected to the thigh bone.
7. The thigh bone connected to the hip bone.

This will happen easily once you have:

- ✓ ensured that the information is there for you to recall (in other words, you need to have learned your subject – more about this in Chapters 4 and 5);
- ✓ stopped any negative runaway thoughts by using the exercises in Chapters 3, 4, 5 and 9;
- ✓ achieved relaxation by using the scripts in Chapters 6 and 7 so that the information recall process will happen automatically.

By relaxing and learning to let go, the process will happen automatically.

TIP

Your subconscious mind stores information because you might need it. It wants you to retrieve this information when it is required. It will help you all it can.

Let's go back to our bike riding example. Your subconscious has kept that information about exactly how to ride a bike safely stored away. Perhaps it's been many years since you have ridden a bike. Yet having a bike in front of you is enough to bring back into your awareness all your knowledge about how to ride one, and off you go.

Chapter 3

Why we want to do well in the exam

The dictionary definition for 'examination' is: 'a formal test of a person's knowledge or proficiency in a subject or skill, by questions oral or written.' Exams have not always existed. The system in the UK allowing every person to have an education has been in place for less than 200 years. Even up until relatively recently, this system was tiered according to social class. A series of Acts of Parliament reformed teaching and the examination process until it arrived at the system we recognise today.

Exams give you great freedom and it's easy to forget this when the exam day is tomorrow and your teacher or lecturer has been telling you for the past year that you have to take it and you have to do well.

Visualise your exams like buttons for levels in a lift. The top floor of the building is your goal. It will take time, experience and hard work, but the reward is there for you: doing what you want to be doing – whether that is becoming a doctor, or a lawyer, or having a career in fashion design, engineering or the building trade. Those certificates and diplomas will show you and everyone else that you have the knowledge, the skill and the training to do well in your chosen career.

You might already be halfway up the building in the lift. You might already have passed the first few floors and now you are at the next stage.

Generally, we can press these lift buttons at the pace that feels right for us. Most of us take our GCSEs in the middle of our teens, we take our A levels in our late teens and if we decide to go to university this happens around the end of our teens. However, there are many of us throughout the country taking these exams or equivalent vocational qualifications at all stages of our lives.

People decide to learn again, to change career direction, or to finally find the time, the motivation or the confidence to work towards what they really want to do. The great thing about exams is that not only are they open to everyone but they disregard age too.

TIP

Even in the unlikely event of you not doing as well as you had hoped in your exams, it is usually easy to retake them or to change direction and to take other exams at another time.

When you are telling yourself 'I must pass', that's only partly true. If you don't, you can generally take the exam again. The education system in this country wants you to pass and it gives you all the chances you might need to do so.

Most of us understand this, and most of us who feel enormous pressure when taking exams are experiencing that pressure for other reasons. Let's take a look at these other reasons and see if you can identify with some of them:

Competitiveness

We naturally compare ourselves to others around us. We use comparisons to make sense of our world and to recognise our own place in it. This external referencing system helps us to recognise whether we are average height or tall, fair or dark, male or female and so on.

Exam results are an external measurement tool too. Having an A level in mathematics might indicate that we are more likely to succeed in a particular job application than someone who doesn't have one. Among our friends and colleagues, having an A grade in A level mathematics might indicate that we worked harder or that we have a better understanding of maths than our classmates who obtained lesser grades.

How will this make us feel? How will we feel if we get a C grade and our closest friend gets an A grade, or vice versa? It could create a feeling of anxiety for us. It might create conflict in our minds. Will our friend lose interest in us or be jealous of our success? Will they feel bad for us because they did better?

Expecting a negative outcome

Are you telling yourself that you expect to do badly? Why set up this expectation for yourself? Our brain cannot actually process negative statements. If you tell yourself 'I know I'll do badly,' you are, in some ways, more likely to do badly than if you tell yourself 'I know I'll do well.' This is because your brain hears the words 'do badly' and can start to act on that message.

Let me give you an example. I'd like you to not think about baked beans. No, I said don't think about baked beans. Are you still thinking about them? Yes, you have to think about the thing that you are trying not to think about.

Seeing negative outcomes of success

Yes, that's right – the negative outcome of success. What if you were to succeed? Supposing that meant you are on the next floor in your lift. What if that means leaving home, going to university; what if that means you might actually achieve your goal?

Feeling useless and put down by others

Self-esteem is how we think of ourselves.

A nice healthy level of self-esteem gives us the confidence in ourselves and our abilities to do the things we want and choose to do.

Our self-esteem level is set at a relatively young age, often before we go to school, and is usually set by the messages we receive from our parents and significant people around us at the time.

Once set, we believe this about ourselves. We'll measure new information against our self-belief and reject anything that doesn't fit. So, if we have grown up thinking that we are not good at things because we were told we were clumsy or useless, then we believe this to be the case. It can make challenges more difficult – not because we are useless, but because subconsciously we keep telling ourselves that we are.

Then, if someone tells us that we are useless, we are more likely to believe them. And, if we tell ourselves that we are useless, then we behave as if we are ('see, I told you I couldn't do it') and others are more likely to treat us the same way. We have set up a negative cycle of events and thoughts that perpetuates our low sense of self-worth.

This has nothing to do with our actual ability. But, it is a sad fact that we do things less well if we believe we are not capable of doing them. Happily for us, the reverse is also true. You do things very well when you believe you are capable of doing them. This book will help you to realise your own capabilities.

Your brain is an amazing thing. The actual structure of our brain is the same for us all, but how we use it makes our individual capabilities different. We know that if we exercise a lot our muscles become stronger. We know that if we exercise certain muscles, then those muscles in particular become stronger. Your brain works on similar principles. You make stronger connections depending on what you are spending most time on. If you ride a bike a lot, your brain is very competent at spatial awareness, distance and balance, and it keeps your eyes and ears finely tuned to what is happening around you. If you read a lot, your brain will become more competent in different areas such as focusing on small text, making sense of the patterns of words, understanding the meaning of the text, and so on.

So let's be clear. Your brain is amazing. In the last chapter I discussed the subconscious mind and how it stores everything that you have learned and experienced. That is a lot of information. If it has also been storing messages that you are useless, and not allowing you to store messages about the things you do well, then you are swimming against the tide.

You will change this negative self-belief by regularly using the script in Chapter 8. For now, have a go at this exercise:

Exercise

Take five minutes to make a list of all the things that you are really good at. Let me help you by putting a few possible items on your list:

- ✓ Seeing things
- ✓ Hearing
- ✓ Ability to talk
- ✓ Digesting food
- ✓ Walking
- ✓ Writing with a pen
- ✓ Using cutlery
- ✓ Opening doors
- ✓ Getting dressed

- ✓ Understanding people's feelings
- ✓ Riding a bike
- ✓ Brushing your hair
- ✓ Writing lists

Need longer than five minutes? Yes, I thought so.

Now, go back through this list and take a moment to realise what an amazing task even the simplest thing on the list really is. Can you imagine what a complex process writing a list is? Can you imagine trying to build a machine that can write and think about what to write as well as you can? You are amazing, aren't you?

Feeling pushed or pulled by others

- 'I've got to take the exams; mum and dad have told me I have to do well'

Our family often want us to do well in exams. Why would this be? Hopefully, it is because they love us a lot and they want to share our joy when we feel happy with the result.

This may be because we come from a family of high achievers and we are expected to do well. It might also be because we have parents who feel that they didn't have the opportunities that we have and they want us to do well because it helps them feel that they have achieved something.

Perhaps we are taking the exam because our brothers and sisters did, or because our friends are. Whatever you perceive the reasons of others to be, ask yourself now, why am *I* taking this exam?

Write down on a piece of paper all of the reasons that you can think of for taking this exam. Then, have a look through the list. Perhaps it looks something like this:

'I have to take the exam to get into college/university/get that job.'
'I must take the exam because my teacher/tutor says I have to.'

'I've got to take the exam because my parents would be disappointed if I didn't.'

'I should take the exam because all my school/college friends are taking it.'

'I must take the exam to pass the course.'

> 'I have to take the exam because it is expected of me to do well.'

Can you see the theme running through these reasons?

Words like 'should', 'must' and 'have' all make us feel as if we are forced to do something. They take away our own control, and yet they are words that we are using ourselves. We are the ones giving the orders here, pushing ourselves in a direction that we don't necessarily want to go. When we feel pushed, we feel both powerless and resentful at the same time.

Exercise

Think of something that you really like, something simple, and then replace the words 'the exam' with this thing that you really like. As an example, I'll use 'wearing favourite boots', but you can use anything you want. Then, those statements become:

> 'I have to wear the boots to get into college/university/get that job.'

> 'I must wear the boots because my teacher/tutor says I have to.'
>
> 'I've got to wear the boots because my parents would be disappointed if I didn't.'
>
> 'I should wear the boots because all my school/college friends are wearing theirs.'
>
> 'I must wear the boots to pass the course.'
>
> 'I have to wear the boots because it is expected of me to have the right footwear.'

I'm rapidly losing interest in wearing those boots now I'm being told so firmly that I have to. But who is doing the telling? It is me. Even so, I no longer feel in control of what shoes I choose to wear. When I simply decide that I want to wear those boots today, I feel good about wearing them:

> 'I choose to wear the boots today.'
> 'I want to wear these boots now.'
> 'I think I'll wear my boots today.'

Now, let's do the exercise again. Supposing your list looks something like this:

'I want to take the exam so that I can get the college place/university place/job that I choose.'

'I choose to take the exam because my teacher/tutor says I can do it.'

'I want to take the exam because my parents are proud that I'm taking it.'

'I choose to take the exam in the same way that my school/college friends are choosing to take it.'

'I want to take the exam because I want to pass this course.'

'I choose to take the exam and I expect to do well.'

Making a positive decision and having a choice gives you control. Feeling in control means that you are not feeling threatened, so there's no need to respond to a threat that isn't there. Feeling in control means feeling calm and relaxed.

Now, let's strengthen that feeling.

You feel most in control when you are making decisions for yourself, not for others.

There are a few reasons on the list above that are for someone else – tutors, friends and parents. Remind yourself now that if these people want to feel good because you are doing well, that's not the same as them feeling good because they are doing well. Ultimately, we are all responsible for creating our own success and it is not down to others to create our feelings of success for us. Yes, it's great to know that our friend has done well in their exam. It's a better feeling knowing that we have done well in our exam. Take your exam for you.

> 'I choose to take the exam and I expect to do well.'

This is a good statement. It recognises that you do have a choice about taking the exam. And, because you feel in a powerful position, you feel calm and confident and you expect to do well.

Chapter 4

Taking charge

Now you know that you have chosen to take the exam, it is time to take charge and create the best possible outcome for you. This is the beginning of a successful strategy that you will have employed before. Think of an example of something that you really want to do. This could be anything nice and simple such as buying a new coat, to perhaps deciding to travel for the summer months. Having decided what it is you really want to do, how do you make it a reality? You plan for it. First you have the idea, you visualise it in your mind, you make it an attractive option, and then you work out how to make it happen. Then, you make it happen.

The process might be something like this:

- ✓ Idea: I want the new coat that I've seen in the shop.
- ✓ Visualise: I see myself wearing the coat and how good I feel in it.
- ✓ Plan: I'm working out how much money I need to buy it;
  working out how much extra I'll need;
  working out how to get the extra cash;
  working out how quickly I can achieve this.
- ✓ I'm buying the coat.

Now that you have decided that you want to take the exam and get a good result, it is time to work out a plan of action to make it a reality.

- ✓ Idea: I want to pass the exam.
- ✓ Visualise: I am taking the exam calmly and confidently and passing it well.
- ✓ Plan: I am working out what I am likely to

be asked in the exam questions;
working out what I need to learn and revise to answer those questions well;
working out the best way to learn and revise my subjects;
working out how I can comfortably achieve this in the time I have available.

- ✓ I am taking the exam and passing it well.

Once you are feeling proactive and confident, you will feel more motivated. Your motivation to buy the new coat is very strong because you are visualising all the benefits of having it. As you see the benefits of taking the exam – in other words, being very pleased with how you have completed it, the successful result and what that will lead to – then your motivation to take the exam naturally increases. When you are motivated, you will do all the necessary preparation that you need to.

TIP

Preparation is what we do constantly throughout our day-to-day lives. Put aside any plans to simply 'wing it' and do that preparation.

Each time you prepare, you will be a step closer to your goal and feeling better about achieving it. The more daily preparation you do, the more confident you will feel about taking the exam. This increased confidence is a reward in itself, but remember to reward yourself often for the preparation that you are doing. Just a small reward will suffice. The best kind of reward is an internal pat on the back. How often do you do this? When was the last time that you took a moment to just sit back and tell yourself that you are doing really well and that the work that you have done is of a high standard?

This only needs to take a minute. It's often the case that we are very good at rewarding everyone else – our pets, young children, our friends and family. We tell them that they have been good, done well, look great and so on, yet often we feel strange about doing this for ourselves. We recognise the importance of other people getting this praise and encouragement, don't we? How does it make them feel?

If you are a dog owner, you'll know how happy and content your dog is if you praise and reward them. Dogs are obvious in their display of feelings and emotions. Their body language clearly demonstrates when they are happy. The same is true of young children. As adults we can learn to hide our feelings more, but that doesn't mean that they are not there. Try this exercise:

Exercise

Take a moment to relax and think about all of the things that you have done today – make a mental list of them. It could be something like:

- ✓ went food shopping
- ✓ cleaned bedroom
- ✓ revised nineteenth century American History
- ✓ planned a night out for Friday

Now, give yourself a moment of praise for each of these. Take a couple of nice deep breaths and tell yourself what a good job you have done. Tell yourself how well you've done everything.

Listen out for negatives:

'I forgot the bread.'

'I should have done it yesterday.'

'I didn't do as much as my friends.'

'I'm still not sure if they want to come.'

Quieten down that negative inner voice and tell it to be silent. We don't have to be perfect in life. Doing 'good enough' is fine.

When you have revised a topic, praise yourself for it and listen to the praise. Quieten the negative inner voice telling you it's not enough and tell yourself firmly that you have done plenty of good work and that you will continue to do so. As you praise yourself, your subconscious mind will be much more interested in doing more good work in the future.

Our subconscious doesn't like doing things for no reward or for punishment. Why would it? So remember to reward yourself with good, positive thoughts and to forget punishing yourself with negative thoughts. If you are imagining a negative outcome to the exam then you are punishing yourself. When you do this, why would you want to work towards that exam?

So, reward yourself. Visualise a good positive outcome to the exam. For example:

'I've revised nineteenth century American History and I feel good about this. I've done well to work on this topic. I know now that when I am asked a question in the exam about this topic I will be pleased because I know how to answer that question well. I'll feel calm and confident and when the exam is finished I will feel really happy and contented knowing that I have done as well as I wanted to.'

In the next chapter I'll be helping you in your approach to the exam. Much of this concerns feeling in control. This feeling is the opposite of feeling nervous.

Chapter 5

Getting prepared

When we feel anxious about something, we use a coping strategy called 'avoidance'. This means that we actively avoid something – either physically or mentally. If you are feeling anxious about exams, then you might be avoiding doing anything connected with them, such as revision, and you may be avoiding thinking about them too.

Avoidance is a natural coping strategy and we all do it to some extent, but it is not a solution to a problem.

TIP

Facing up to our fears and anxieties is the way to overcome them.

You are reading this book because you want to overcome your exam anxiety, so let's do that right now. Now, face your fears and tell yourself firmly that you are going to take the exam, you are going to do well and you are certainly going to pass. Now really say it.

Exercise

Repeat out loud:

'I am taking the exam.'
'I will do well in the exam.'
'I am certainly going to pass the exam.'

If you are taking more than one exam, repeat this exercise for each one.

Good, now you have an intention, next you can work on a plan. Don't be concerned at this moment that those nerves are still there. They will be getting calmer from this moment forward. Using your plan, your intentions and the exercises in this book, you will be feeling calm and focused for your exam.

As soon as you stop avoiding, you can formulate a positive plan to achieve anything you want. We do this all the time. Think of something that you really wanted to do in the past and then did it. It can be anything: riding a bike, travelling to Nepal, moving house. Once you had the intention and started focusing on it, a plan then came naturally into action. This plan did not just involve the actual details, but also lots of ways where you found yourself quite naturally working towards your goal.

It's much easier to work towards your goal if you know what it is.

It is, after all, much easier for footballers to score a goal once the goalposts are in place and the team know where the area called 'goal' is. Then, the team naturally keep moving the ball towards that place. You'll do the same now that you have a goal in place.

You may already have the exact dates for your exam or an idea of when it might be. Now you can start to really move towards that goal and prepare. This means putting into place a multi-faceted action plan that will involve the following:

- ✓ Knowing your subject
- ✓ Knowing what is expected
- ✓ Increasing your skills and capabilities
- ✓ Increasing your calm, focus and confidence

Knowing your subject

You have already been reading in a previous chapter how you store information, and how you will be able to retrieve this information by way of short reminders (remember our knee bone connected to the thigh bone example?). Of course, if you don't put the information into your memory in the first place, you won't have anything to remember.

If you have difficulty understanding a particular subject or aspect of a subject, stop avoiding it and seek help and advice now.

Your teacher or tutor would be happy to help, or you could seek extra tutoring – again, your college could help with this. Friends and study groups may help too. Do start by talking to your teacher or tutor. Often a brief chat and some guidance will be all you need to gain the necessary understanding.

It is no use reading something again and again if you really don't understand the information that you are reading. It's much better to take some time to really figure it out. Often, trying to think of an example is helpful, or using a metaphor, or even working out some physical way of demonstrating it. Mathematical problems, for example, are often much easier to understand if you can draw them out on a piece of paper or use something physical that you can count or divide.

So, take charge, take action and seek advice if there is something you don't understand. Remember, your teacher or tutor wants you to pass the exam. They will do what they can to help. Don't feel embarrassed if you have to admit that you don't know something. A teacher can often find it very difficult to realise if a class of attentive students really understands what is being taught. Unless the teacher gets feedback, how can they know? So remember, they are here to teach you and that's what they want to do. If you have a problem with something, ask for help.

Now, put together a revision plan. Hopefully you have notes and textbooks that you can return to and revise. Revision is essential and is best done as part of a firm plan to ensure you have time to revise all the information that you will need. Put together a timetable and stick to it. Ensure that you have time within that plan to do other things that you need to do, and remind yourself that you may need to put some things on hold until after the exam.

Each time you revise a topic, give yourself a reward. Not something spectacular, just a moment of recognition that you are another step closer to your goal and that you have worked hard. Don't just give yourself the reward by telling yourself, but allow yourself to hear it. Sit quietly for a moment and try this out:

Take a moment now to congratulate yourself for taking positive action by reading this book. Tell yourself that you have done a good thing, something that is moving you closer to your goal of feeling calm, focused and comfortable in the exam and passing it well. If this feels strange, that's OK – it's something we are not used to doing. Now, give yourself a moment to really feel that praise. Let it be a nice, comfortable, warm feeling that brings a smile to your face. If any negative thoughts creep in, dismiss them quickly and keep with the comfortable feeling. If you find this uncomfortable, do it again until it feels fine. Now, remind yourself to do this each time you complete part of your revision plan.

Knowing what is expected

Now that you have stopped avoidance tactics, you can pay close attention to what is expected of you in the exam. Look through any information you have, ask questions that you might have and ensure that you have all the information you need. Knowing what is expected might include knowing the answers to the following points:

- ✓ When is the exam?
- ✓ What subjects will it cover?
- ✓ Do I have to answer all the questions? If not, how many?

- ✓ Is it multiple choice?
- ✓ Do I have to answer the questions in the order they are written?
- ✓ How long is the exam?
- ✓ How long will I have to answer each question?
- ✓ What should I take into the exam with me?
- ✓ What am I allowed to take into the exam with me?
- ✓ Do I show my rough notes and workings on the exam paper?
- ✓ Is it better to answer part of a question if I don't know all of the answer?
- ✓ When will I have the results?

Being prepared will ensure that you keep your level of anxiety down to a minimum and feel much more in control. If you know, for example, that you don't have to answer the questions in order, you can answer the question that you feel most confident about first, which will boost your self-confidence and improve your recall of information during the exam.

Increasing your skills and capabilities

By setting yourself a plan, you will overcome obstacles and, by keeping to a revision plan, you will be increasing your skills and capabilities. Focusing on the goal and not using avoidance will also prove beneficial.

TIP

Look after your general health and well-being. They are major factors in helping you to stay alert and focused.

It is now well known that poor diet and lifestyle will affect academic performance in a negative way, so do what you can to make some simple changes.

Start by working on a healthy, varied diet of fresh vegetables, fruits, grains and pulses and increase your intake of nutritious foods; perhaps supplement this with a multivitamin and mineral tablet each day. Just a few changes to your diet can strongly increase your levels of concentration, understanding and retention of information. If necessary, a nutritionist can help you with a plan. Otherwise, there are many good books available. If you have any medical issues that are affected by your diet, have a chat with your doctor for advice.

Don't make the mistake of trying to cram in extra study hours by increasing caffeine or sugary foods and drinks. Substances such as coffee, strong tea, fizzy drinks and cigarettes can certainly increase your feelings of anxiety. They may keep you awake, but they will do nothing for your focus, your concentration or your recall. It is much better to eat well and cut down on cigarettes, coffee, tea and alcohol.

Get plenty of exercise and rest. You may protest that you need a lot of time to revise and study. Yes, that might be true, but you need quality revision and study time, rather than being dog tired and gazing blankly at your notes.

TIP

Ten minutes of good quality revision time gives a strong understanding of the subject and is always better than staying up to the small hours poring over text books when nothing is sinking in.

Exercise not only keeps you physically healthy but mentally healthy too. It releases endorphins into your system, which allow you to feel happy and relaxed. Exercise does not have to be something major. Increase your exercise time by just being more active. Walking is a great form of exercise and I strongly recommend it. The simple, repetitive motion has a calming effect on the mind as well as being an easy form of exercise – get into the habit of taking small, five-to-ten minute walking breaks between study periods.

And finally, get plenty of sleep. Not just on the night before the exam: aim to get plenty of sleep from now on. You might find that playing your recordings of the scripts in Chapters 7 and 8 last thing at night will help you to have a good night's sleep.

TIP

Remember: sleep is essential for your well-being. When you are tired you don't do anything as well as when you are properly rested.

If getting plenty of sleep means cutting down on those evenings out, then make this part of your plan. Your exams are important to you, aren't they?

Increasing your sense of calm, focus and confidence

The final part of your plan is to improve your general levels of calm, focus and confidence. I mention this last in the chapter because everything that you have been reading about so far has been geared towards this. Having a plan, working through issues, being prepared and feeling fit and healthy will make you feel calm, relaxed and confident about your exam. Taking action and not avoiding the issue will do this too.

Feeling much stronger? Good. Now you are ready for the rest of this book, which has easy-to-follow exercises for further increasing your sense of calm, focus and self-confidence.

Chapter 6

Working with the scripts

The rest of this book contains a series of scripts and exercises for you to use. They will help you to reduce significantly any experience of anxiety that you might be feeling, and they will in turn help you feel much more relaxed about your exam.

The most important of these is contained in the next chapter. It is a script that you need to listen to and I will explain how you need to do this. It is a hypnotherapy script that allows you to make changes comfortably and easily to the way you have been thinking about the exam. The script is entirely safe and comfortable to use, and once prepared is easy to work with. Do take the time to prepare it. This script uses the same principles that I have been applying in my therapy practice with many hundreds of clients. This is your opportunity to use these principles for yourself.

How the script works

Earlier on in this book I talked to you about expectations. If you expect or believe that you will pass your exam well, you are more likely to do so.

One powerful way that our mind believes a positive result is possible is if we have had experience of this outcome before.

If you have visualised yourself calmly passing the exam, you are more likely to believe that you will pass with confidence.

Those of you who have already passed an exam will believe more strongly that you can pass the next one. The script will instil this same belief. It works with you at a subconscious level so you do not even have to think much about what it is saying. Keep in mind the letting-go of conscious control that was discussed previously.

Each time you play the script, you will subconsciously believe more and more that you can take your exam in a relaxed, calm and focused way, and that you will pass it well.

Preparing the script

The script needs to be recorded or read to you – rather than read by you. When listening to the words you need to be able to lie back quietly and undisturbed with your eyes closed. You need to do this as many times as you can before your exam.

Simply reading the words in this chapter will not have the desired effect – you need to make a recording of the script. Once the recording is completed, you are free to play the script as often as you like.

How you record the script is entirely up to you. A cassette tape, digital or CD recording will all be equally effective as long as your voice is clear enough.

If you find it impossible to record the script yourself, then you will need to enlist the help of a friend or relative who will be willing to read the words to you while you relax – do ensure that they realise that they will need to do this regularly.

When to play the script

Once you have your recording, play the script regularly right up to the day of your exam. Understand that the recording you have made is a basic relaxation script, so it may make you feel drowsy or even fall asleep.

For this reason, it is vital that you *never* play it when you are driving, or in a car where another driver can hear it.

Play the script from beginning to end undisturbed – do not play it if you know someone is phoning you in five minutes, or the dinner has to be ready in 20 minutes.

Find yourself free time every day to play the script, and always play it through to the end.

If you find the recording makes you fall asleep, don't worry. Your subconscious is still receiving the message. Use the script at bedtime if you wish.

The ideal time to start working with the script is around three weeks before your exam. If your exam is less than three weeks away, do not worry; any time that you can play the script will have some benefit for you so just start the work as soon as you can.

How to play the script

Get into a comfortable position, either sitting or lying down. Make sure that you are warm and will be undisturbed by others – unplug the telephone if you need to.

Now, simply rest and turn on your recording. Headphones are better than speakers if you can arrange this.

Close your eyes and listen to the words. Don't try to pay attention too closely, just listen and follow the instructions.

If you find yourself drifting off – that's fine. If you find yourself thinking about other things, gently bring your awareness back to the recording.

After listening to your recording, you will feel calm and relaxed. This is a pleasant feeling and one to be enjoyed. With today's hectic lifestyles, it's all too difficult to give ourselves time to relax, but when we do, we feel enormous benefits from it. Over time, this type of relaxation can lower our blood pressure, and boost our immune system so that we suffer fewer colds and coughs. We also find that we have more energy and can concentrate more effectively.

Recording the script

When recording the script, speak clearly and slowly, emphasising any important words or phrases. Take your time. Leave gaps between the sentences. Imagine that you are reading a bedtime story to a young child. When we are relaxed, we sometimes think more slowly, and it is good that the script is in pace with this relaxation. Use a soothing tone of voice, keeping the words spoken quietly, not rushed.

Everybody's speech speed is different, but the recorded script is intended to be around 30 minutes long. If your recording lasts only 20 minutes, then you have rushed through this important preparation process; give yourself another go so that you are doing as much as possible to promote your own relaxation.

Exercise

Try reading this test passage. It will help you to establish the right pace of reading before you record your script.

When you are ready, take a glance at the clock and then read aloud the following passage. It should take you around two minutes to do so. If you are reading it in less than two minutes, go back over it until you have slowed down sufficiently.

The dots between words are an indication of gaps to leave when you are speaking. Put emphasis on the words in capitals.

Test passage

'... From THIS MOMENT FORWARD... I know that I AM GETTING BETTER AND BETTER... From this moment forward... I KNOW... that I am MORE CONFIDENT, MORE RELAXED AND MORE CALM whenever I think about my exam...This is because... I am better prepared... and because I understand better... why I have been feeling... the way that I have... I know now... that MY THOUGHTS... AND FEELINGS... AND ACTIONS... ARE PERFECTLY... WITHIN MY CONTROL... I know... that on the day of my exam... I will feel REALLY GOOD, REALLY CALM AND CONFIDENT... I know... that on the day of my exam... I will do REALLY WELL... because I CAN DO REALLY WELL... I know that ON THE DAY OF MY EXAM... I WILL BE CONFIDENT... AND CALM AND FOCUSED because I am already growing my inner calmness... and confidence and focus every day in every way... EVERY DAY... IN EVERY WAY... I AM BECOMING MORE CALM... AND MORE CONFIDENT... AND MORE FOCUSED and because I am becoming... calmer and more focused and more confident... I know that I am able to do so much more.'

Get the idea? Now use the same pace and emphasis of speaking when you are recording the exam script, nice and clearly.

Chapter 7

Relaxation script for sitting the exam

'Now... just sitting or lying back with your eyes gently closed... just allow yourself to get into a nice, comfortable position so that you can really relax.

You don't have to do anything at all now... just simply listen and let your mind wander... you don't have to do anything at all except listen to these words.

This is a very pleasant and relaxing feeling. Listening to these words will help you to feel really relaxed.

Now, keeping your eyes closed... just concentrate on your body for a moment... Allow all the muscles in your body to really, really relax... Take a mental journey through your body now... so that you can allow all the muscles in your body to relax... This is a very comfortable and pleasant feeling... and you can just let it happen... Let it happen in its own time... in your own way.

So... start with your feet and toes now... Concentrate for a moment on your feet and toes ... and as you do so allow all the muscles in your feet and your toes to really relax... Let those muscles relax and go soft and stretch out... A very pleasant feeling... Now allow this pleasant feeling of relaxation to move further up your legs... into your ankles and your calves... Let all those muscles really relax... Stretching and softening.

Now take that feeling of deep relaxation... further up into your knees and your thighs... so that all the muscles in your legs are really relaxing... A very pleasant and calming sensation... and as you become more physically relaxed... so you become more mentally relaxed as well... and you can just let your mind wander in its own unique way...

Now move that feeling of relaxation up... into the muscles of your hips, your buttocks and your lower back and stomach... Feel all those muscles really relaxing... A very pleasant and comfortable feeling... Very pleasant and comfortable.

Now move that feeling of relaxation further up... into the muscles of your middle and upper back, and your chest... Allow those muscles to really stretch out and relax... and as this happens... very naturally... so your breathing can become deeper... and longer... and more relaxed... Let all those muscles really relax.

Now take that feeling of relaxation... into the muscles of your arms, and your hands... so that all the muscles in your upper arms, your forearms... your wrists and your hands are really relaxing... A very pleasant and comfortable feeling... Now take that feeling of relaxation into the muscles of your shoulders and your neck... Let those muscles of your shoulders and your neck... really soften, stretch, and relax... Very comfortable...

Now take that feeling of relaxation up... from your neck to your chin, your jaw, and your head... All the muscles of your face... your mouth... your cheeks... your nose... around your eyes... and your forehead... Really, really relaxing... Now take that feeling of relaxation... to the muscles of your scalp... the top of your head... the back and sides of your head... allowing all those muscles to completely relax... to soften... and really relax...

Now all the muscles in your entire body are relaxed... and this is a very pleasant and comfortable feeling... and you can just lie or sit there... so relaxed... and so comfortable... just listening to these words...

Now that you are feeling much more physically relaxed... so you are feeling more mentally relaxed too... And with this feeling of relaxation... comes a really lovely sense of calm and tranquillity... Calm... Calm... Say the word through your mind... and as you say the word through your mind... so you experience that wonderful feeling of calm and tranquillity.

As you are relaxing now... take a moment of time to think about the preparation that you are doing to pass your exam...The preparation that you are doing not just to pass your exam but to pass your exam really well... Already... you are feeling so in control... so focused and so confident about the exam because you know that you will do really well... And you know that each time you revise a topic... each time you read through your notes... each time you spend time thinking about the subject... you feel even more in control and even more focused... This is an exciting time... You like to plan and to have control over how your plans will work out and this plan is all so beautifully simple.

You have accepted the challenge of taking your exam and now you feel so good about that challenge... An opportunity to show your knowledge and understanding... An opportunity to test your own skills and knowledge knowing that your level of skill and knowledge is high and grows higher every day... From this moment forward you are thinking more and more clearly... focusing more and more clearly... everything is becoming easier and easier... Everything is becoming easier in every way... Your mind... alert and focused... your thinking sharp and clear... your memory stronger and better... You find that the more you study and revise... the clearer your mind becomes... the stronger your memory becomes... You are finding it so easy... day by day... to understand... to learn and to retain all the information you are learning and revising... it is all so beautifully simple.

And because you are finding it all so easy... you are enjoying your learning and your revising... you are more interested in your subject than you have ever been... You are discovering new understandings and new information about your subject each day... And because you are discovering new understandings and new information... you are remembering so much more... retaining so much more... Your subject is so very clear to you and your understanding of your subject is high... And as you revise... you find that time moves at just the right speed... so that you have all the time you need to revise and learn your topic within your study period... And at the end of your study period you rest... feeling completely satisfied... filled with knowledge and understanding... retaining that information within your memory and this feels so relaxing and so good.

And as each day goes by and your knowledge grows stronger and deeper... and your subject becomes clearer and clearer to you... you move closer to taking your exam... and this feels so good... an opportunity to show your knowledge... your chance to make all your work and revision worthwhile... As your exam comes closer... you feel brimming with knowledge and understanding in a very focused and clear way and you know that you are ready... And this readiness feels so good... a natural clarity and confidence deep within you... A confidence that is strong and bright and powerful... reminding you of all the things that you have done when you have felt this same confidence.

And with this confidence comes a wonderful sense of inner calm... An inner calm that is the inner calm that you feel when you have knowledge... when you have mastery... when you have expertise... When you feel this inner calm everything happens so easily... everything is so comfortable... you feel completely in control... And you feel this inner calm now... as the exam approaches... because you know that you are ready... and you know that you are passing this exam... comfortably and easily and you are passing this exam well.

And as the exam comes closer and it is the night before the exam... you know that you are so confident and so relaxed... A wonderful inner relaxation that spreads right through you... A relaxation that you feel from the very centre of your being... no matter how alert or focused or active you need to be... an inner relaxation that allows you to feel so confident... ready to tackle any challenge easily and comfortably and confidently.

And because you feel this wonderful inner relaxation... you find yourself sleeping easily and comfortably and deeply on the night before your exam... You have been sleeping easily and comfortably in all the previous days and weeks and this night is no exception... You rest and you sleep soundly and comfortably and as you sleep your inner mind... that deep inner part of you... is reminding you that you are ready and confident and so calm about your exam... it all feels so easy.

And upon sleeping soundly and comfortably... you awake on the morning of your exam completely refreshed and revived and feeling wonderful... You give yourself some time to relax while you are awake... because you have plenty of time... And you feel so wonderfully confident and focused... your mind clear and sharp... your memory active... and you are ready to share your knowledge and understanding in the exam.

Time passes so comfortably... you are so well prepared... and feeling calm... relaxed and filled with confidence... you are ready to make your way to the exam... You do so... easily... comfortably and arrive at the exam venue feeling refreshed... relaxed and yet alert... calm and yet focused... Feeling relaxed... calm and confident... You are completely focused on the task ahead... ready and looking forward to starting... feeling comfortable and feeling relaxed.

Time passes so comfortably now and soon you find yourself sitting at your seat... listening easily and comfortably to the instructions that you are given... Feeling relaxed and calm and confident... you allow yourself to prepare... laying out your pens, pencils, stationery and other instruments... You feel yourself taking a nice steady breath and you hear yourself saying the word "calm" through your mind... As you do so you feel a wonderful sense of inner calm and confidence spreading comfortably and deeply through every part of you... mind and body... Enjoying the feeling... you know that you are ready... ready to complete this exam comfortably and easily.

When instructed... you easily and comfortably turn the paper and read the questions... Within you... a deep feeling of calm and relaxation... With ease... you realise that you have all the answers... all the knowledge... to complete this exam easily and well... You take your time to focus... feeling wonderfully confident and relaxed... your confidence growing moment by moment as you calmly and slowly read the instructions and the questions... Calmly and confidently... completely focused... you formulate your plan... your plan of how you are answering these questions... in what order... how much time you will take on each... It's all so easy... so beautifully easy and you are so confident and calm because you are doing so well... Making any checks that you need to check... you find yourself answering the questions easily and comfortably... the information that you need is right there every moment that you need it... ready to transfer it from your memory to your written answer... clearly... concisely and accurately.

Your answers are clear... you are amazed at how much information you are retrieving... surprising yourself at how much you really know... how much knowledge you have stored within your memory... within your understanding... And this amazement brings with it a wonderful feeling of deep inner calm... and a wonderful confidence... strong and powerful... And the more calm and confidence you feel... the more you realise that you know... The more you retrieve your knowledge to write your answers clearly and concisely... the more you realise you know... And your answers are flowing easily... comfortably... and you feel so relaxed.

Time is passing easily and comfortably now... just at the right pace for you... You have all the time you need to answer your questions in the way that you want to answer them... There is no rush... you are relaxed and focused... Your writing is easy and fluid... transferring your thoughts and ideas to your writing on the page... All so comfortable... and you feel that wonderful inner feeling of calm and confidence... That wonderful feeling of focus and clarity...

You take a moment to see the information that you are writing... it is all so beautifully clear... so well written and explained... so well laid out and clear... As you write... you can perhaps hear the information through your mind... your ideas coming into your mind clearly and concisely... hearing those ideas... transferring that information to the page.

And time passes now and you realise that you have finished saying everything that you want to say... You have formulated your answers to say everything that you know you needed to say to answer those questions... You realise that you have a few minutes left and you feel so wonderfully calm and relaxed... Feeling focused and completely confident... you take those moments to just read through your work... making any last-moment, fine adjustments... ensuring that you have done everything that you needed to do... but you already know that you have... Feeling calm and relaxed... you hear the examiner saying that the exam is now complete... With a wonderful feeling of confidence and pride you put down your pen or pencil... tidy your exam paper and realise that you have finished...

Feeling so confident... so calm and so relaxed... you take a moment to rest and relax... You feel so good... you know that you have done so very well... You take a few deep breaths and allow the muscles in your body to completely relax... You have worked hard and you deserve this moment of complete physical and mental relaxation... Feeling so pleased... so relaxed... so happy and so confident... when you are told that you can... you leave the exam room with a wonderful feeling of inner calm and inner relaxation... You admit to yourself that you enjoyed that experience... You enjoyed that opportunity to focus and realise just how much knowledge you really have and you are enjoying this moment now... Smiling... you take a moment to enjoy this feeling... As you walk from the room you feel strong and calm and focused and confident... A feeling that you keep with you... because this feeling is entirely for your benefit... and your inner mind understands that this feeling is entirely for your benefit.

Time moves forward now... let time move forward in your mind... You realise now that you have the results of your exam... Feeling confident and calm... reminding yourself of how well you already know you have done... it comes as no surprise to discover that yes... you really have done well... Even better than you even expected to do... You feel a strong feeling of joyfulness and confidence move through every part of you as you realise that the result is even better than you expected... You see that result clearly in front of you now... seeing that very positive result... You feel so good... you can see yourself smiling... happy... joyful and filled with confidence... You take this moment to congratulate yourself and you feel the joy of your own reward... This is a wonderful feeling... This is a moment that you will remember often... this moment of pride... this moment of success... This moment that is entirely for your benefit... You hold onto this moment and you savour this moment and you hear yourself telling yourself through your mind "well done" because you know that you have really done well... And from this moment forward... you know that whenever you set yourself a challenge like an exam... that you accept and you meet that challenge... and this feels so inwardly calm and you feel so focused and relaxed and confident... You know now that from this moment forward you accept the challenge of exams easily... comfortably in this way... And you know now that any exam that you take in the future is easy and comfortable for you because you accept the challenge... you prepare well and when you take the exam your knowledge comes into your awareness easily and comfortably as you need it to... And because you feel this way... any time you take an exam in the future... you always feel so inwardly calm... so focused and relaxed and confident and this is a good feeling.

Take a moment to relax with this feeling now... to completely relax... and let this feeling and understanding sink into a nice deep part of your memory along with all your other knowledge and understanding... feeling so comfortable there.

Relax now for a few moments more... savouring this feeling... In a few moments' time I'll count from one to three and say "open your eyes"... When I do... you'll become fully wide awake and alert and feel completely ready to carry on with the rest of your day feeling very much better than before... Ready now to hear me count... so counting now... one... two... three and open your eyes... Now fully wide awake and refreshed.'

Chapter 8

General relaxation and confidence script

When you have played your recording of the exam script a few times you will notice that it makes you feel very good. The relaxation that it helps you to maintain has positive effects on other areas of your life as well as benefits specific to your exam. You will find that it has a lasting effect on your everyday levels of relaxation and calmness.

Below is a general confidence and relaxation script. Several of my clients use recordings of similar scripts between hypnotherapy sessions. It is always good to find time for ourselves when we can simply relax. Playing a recording of this script regularly can be helpful in reducing general stress levels.

While you are preparing for your exam, you can record this script and play it as well as your exam script if you wish, perhaps alternating them on a daily basis.

Of course, once you have passed your exam, you will have no need to play the exam script, but you can keep using the script in this chapter.

The script

'Now... just sitting or lying back with your eyes gently closed... just listening to the sound of my voice... just allow yourself to get into a nice comfortable position so that you can really relax.

You don't have to do anything at all now... just simply listen and let your mind wander...

You don't have to move... although you may if you want to... and you don't have to talk... You don't have to do anything at all except listen to these words.

This is a very pleasant and relaxing feeling... You can just let go and feel really relaxed... Listening to these words will help you to feel really relaxed.

Now... keeping your eyes closed... just focus on your body for a moment... Allow all the muscles in your body to really relax... Take a mental journey through your body now... so that you can allow all the muscles in your body... to really relax... This is a very comfortable and pleasant feeling... and you can just allow yourself... to let it happen... Let it happen in its own time... in your own way.

As you are doing this... just allow yourself now... to begin to focus your attention inwards... so you can just begin to let your mind drift... Drift as in a pleasant daydream... just letting go of your day-to-day concerns... and allowing your mind to drift towards more pleasant thoughts... More relaxed thoughts... more gentle thoughts...

Imagine now... in your mind's eye... that you are standing on a beautiful beach... A really beautiful beach... Give yourself some time now... to really see this beach... and to grow this picture in your mind... Whatever picture comes to mind... allow yourself to grow this picture in your mind... Whatever you find most beautiful about this beach... allow yourself to grow this in your mind's eye... Notice the colour of the sky and if there are any clouds... Allow yourself some time now to look at the sky... noticing how calm and relaxed... and happy it makes you feel... Now notice the water... its colour... its stillness or movement... and allow yourself to look out across it... as far as you can see... Notice where the sea meets the sky... at the horizon... and how distant and hazy or clear that is.

Feel in your mind's eye... the ground beneath your feet... Whether this is sandy... or rocky... hard or soft... and sense its warmth or coolness... dryness or dampness... and how this feels to you... so good, so relaxing... Feeling now the temperature of the place... its warmth or coolness... whether there is a breeze... or whether the air is warm and still... lazy, serene...

As you feel these sensations... so you notice that this place is so deeply relaxing... so deeply comfortable... and how relaxed and comfortable you are feeling... Take a nice deep breath... and sense any aromas that you can smell... Perhaps the freshness of the air... or the lovely deep smell of the sea... As you notice this... you are feeling even more comfortable and relaxed... It is as if you are breathing in the calmness... and relaxation... of this lovely place with each breath you are taking.

Now allow yourself... as you continue to grow this picture in your mind's eye... to tune into any sounds that you can hear on this beach... Perhaps distant sounds... or the sound of a gentle breeze blowing... Perhaps the sound of the tide ebbing and flowing... back and forth... a gentle ebbing and flowing of the ocean... back and forth... so serene... the rhythm of the ocean... enhancing your feelings of calm and relaxation... enhancing your feelings of serenity.

Now... allow yourself some time... to look around... at anything else that you can see in this very beautiful place... Perhaps there are cliffs or mountains... that rise at the sides... perhaps there are trees or vegetation... Perhaps there are beautiful objects... stones and shells to examine and to explore... Perhaps there are boats at sea... that you can see bobbing... or moving gently, smoothly on the ocean.

Really allow yourself... time to explore this environment... As you do so... really allow yourself... to tune in to the beauty... and the tranquillity of the place... To feel it... to feel its essence... feel its sensations... Feel how relaxed... and peaceful this place is... and feel how relaxed... and peaceful...

you feel in this place... The more time you spend... use all your senses... to truly experience... the peacefulness of the place... and as you do so... you feel a wonderful sense... of deep relaxation... and calmness... This deep relaxation... is so powerful that it is growing stronger... and stronger... as each moment goes by... With it comes a deep sense... of confidence... and calmness... that is growing stronger... and stronger now... with each breath you take... This confidence... and this calmness... will remain long after this relaxation session... This confidence and calmness... will grow stronger and stronger within you... as each moment goes by... Day after day... moment after moment... week after week... this confidence and calmness... increasing in strength... and in depth... moment by moment... You feel so good... so strong... so joyful... and so confident.... No matter where you are... no matter what you are doing... no matter whom you are with... Feeling confident and calm... day after day... stronger and stronger.

Now... as you grow the picture of this lovely environment... this lovely beach... allow yourself... to focus in on one aspect of it... and allow yourself to notice... what it is about this aspect... that is so lovely... so wonderful... Perhaps you would like to focus today... on the movement of the sea... or perhaps the brightness of the sky... Whatever you decide to focus on... you are noticing now what it is... about this aspect... that is so wonderful and so beautiful... and so powerful... As you notice this... and as you recognise this... you are noticing this quality within yourself... You are feeling now... within yourself... your own strength... or beauty... or rhythm... or brightness... whatever that quality is... that you are noticing in the one aspect of this beautiful environment... Each time you listen to these words... you can focus on different aspects... or the same aspect... The choice is yours... Always you will be able to notice... and tune into that truly wonderful positive aspect... and to feel... to feel deeply within you... how that positive aspect relates to you... To feel your own sense of serenity... your own sense of beauty... your own sense of power... your own sense of purpose... your own sense of connection to everything else... or whatever else you are feeling in this moment... as you feel connected to that one aspect of this lovely place.

As you are doing so... you grow within you a wonderful feeling... of calmness... and serenity... as each moment goes by... and in turn... you grow within you strong sensations... of confidence... and calmness... that stay with you as each day goes by.

Now... as you listen to these words... allow yourself a few more moments... of deep relaxation in this very special place.

Now... slowly, gradually... allow yourself to let the image and experience of this lovely, beautiful place... just fade within your memory... so that you can remember it for another time... when you are relaxing once more... As the lovely beach fades into your memory... you notice that the lovely feelings that you are experiencing... are staying with you... so that when you have finished listening to these words... you will still be feeling confident... calm... and joyful... for a long time after.

Rest for a few more moments... Take your time now... becoming aware that you have been in deep relaxation and giving yourself time to orient yourself back to your own environment... In a few moments' time... I shall count to three and as I count... you will become fully awake and fully alert and completely ready to carry on with your day... Then I shall tell you to open your eyes and you will open your eyes and be ready to carry on with your day feeling alert and awake and calm and confident. As you continue listening to these words you know now that the time is coming very quickly when you are ready to open your eyes and be fully awake once more, fully back to full conscious awareness now. Beginning to count now... one... two... and three knowing now that you are fully wide awake and open your eyes.'

Chapter 9

Thinking in the positive

What is the difference between telling yourself 'I will pass the exam' and 'I won't fail the exam'? Telling yourself the first statement is more likely to help you pass the exam. Why? Because our subconscious hears the words 'pass' in the first sentence, but it hears the word 'fail' in the second sentence.

Likewise, if we tell ourselves 'I'll be calm and focused in the exam' that is much better than telling ourselves 'I won't be stressed and nervous in the exam.' Can you sense the difference in these two statements?

TIP

The words that we use throughout our day-to-day lives have a big impact on our thinking and feelings.

Hold on a moment, you might be saying, surely it is the other way around? Surely our thinking and feeling have a big impact on our language? Yes, both are true. There is a strong connection between them. As language is our consciously heard representation of our thoughts and feelings, we can become aware of the language we are using. And, if we make subtle changes to our day-to-day language, we will change our thoughts.

Exercise

Negative thoughts are those that are concerned with what we don't want. Make a list of negative statements that you find yourself using. Often we use them regularly without thinking about it, starting with telling people we're 'not bad' if they ask us how we are.

Examples might be:

'I don't want to feel nervous.'

'I hope I don't miss the bus.'

'I'll try not to mess that up today.'

'Things aren't going too badly.'

'Mind you don't trip on that step there.'

Take a look at your list. Read it through a few times. How do those statements make you feel? Often, when we think about them, we realise that they make us feel a bit miserable, negative and anxious. Looking at my list above, I seem to be spending my life hoping that things don't go wrong, hoping to avoid errors and accidents. That's not a very comfortable way to live, is it?

Why does this happen? It's because what our subconscious is hearing is:

'... nervous.'

'... miss the bus.'

'... mess up.'

'... badly.'

'... trip.'

Let's change the above statements into positive ones:

'I want to be calm.'

'I hope I'm on time for the bus.'

'I'll do that well today.'

'Keep going, you're doing fine.'

'Tread carefully.'

Sometimes, we can even reinforce our negative statements:

'I **know** I'll never pass the exam.'

'I'm **completely** useless at maths.'

'It's **bound** to all go wrong.'

'I'm **addicted** to chocolate.'

'I'll **just die** if he doesn't ask me out.'

These reinforcement words like 'bound' and 'know' have the effect of sealing the fate of the thought. If we tell ourselves that we 'know' we will never pass the exam, then there is certainty of failure. Then, subconsciously, we might feel the need to act upon that certainty. If you are using statements like this, ask yourself, 'What is the evidence?' Have you looked into the future and seen your mark written on the exam paper? No, you haven't, have you?

When predicting the future, all we can say is that the future is uncertain. Uncertain might mean that there is a 50/50 chance of us doing well in the exam. That's hardly the same as *knowing* that we won't pass, is it? Recognising this position allows you to do many things to improve your chance of success. By revising well, your chances of passing well are very high – perhaps even 100 per cent.

The curriculum that you have been working to will ensure that you have covered all the topics that will appear in your exam. Your exams are not going to involve you sitting at a table and having no idea what will be asked of you. You already have a pretty good idea. You know that if you are sitting a maths exam that you will be asked questions about maths. In most cases, you will have studied a curriculum that you will be examined on, so you will even know what kind of maths questions you will be asked. That means that it is relatively easy to push your chances of passing well up to 100 per cent if you learn and revise properly.

You already know this, don't you? So if you are reinforcing your negative statements which you clearly know are inaccurate, then ask yourself why.

One reason we do this is because of those around us. It can gain us attention to talk about our anxieties and concerns. It can help us bond together – a group of friends might find support from each other if they can all appear to be very nervous about the exams. Is this happening for you? Are you with a group of friends who are all negatively discouraging themselves and each other?

> 'Oh, it's going to be awful, I'll never pass.'
>
> 'Me neither, I haven't revised a thing.'
>
> 'I know what you mean; I wish I didn't have to do it.'
>
> 'Me too, I'm thinking of not turning up.'

It's a strange kind of support, isn't it? It feels comforting in a way when our friends are feeling the same way as we are. We can take comfort in the fact that it's not just us that feels nervous. However, this is really unhelpful. What is happening here is that this group of friends is encouraging anxiety and failure, and that is not supportive.

Visualise the best possible outcome

Imagine yourself in, say, 20 years' time. You have achieved everything you want to. In your visualisation, you meet up with your group of friends, for a coffee perhaps. What's the best possible outcome? May I suggest that the best possible outcome is that you meet for coffee regularly with your friends because you are all still in touch. You have all succeeded in everything that you wanted to do and you all know that. You are successful and still friends partly because you are all positive and encourage each other. You all recognise each other's unique talents and abilities and you have all gained from each other's unique talents and abilities – and of course you have gained from your own.

How would this outcome happen? Wind it back 20 years to the present. Now visualise you all in the present meeting for a coffee. It doesn't make sense to have you all sitting there speaking negatively about yourselves It is more likely that you will be saying something like:

'I think we are all going to do all right you know.'

> 'Yes, after all, we know the questions.'
>
> 'I agree. I'm looking forward to it.'
>
> 'Me too, after all, it's getting us all where we want to be.'

Give yourself a few choices here. If you have a group of friends or colleagues who are thinking negatively about the exam, you might need to distance yourself from them just a little in order to release yourself from this web of negativity.

Alternatively, you could be the person to turn this group negativity around and help everyone to think in the positive so that you are all supporting each other in a healthy way.

> 'Hey, come on, I think we're all going to pass you know.'
>
> 'No, I'll never pass.'
>
> 'No, honestly, we all can easily if we just put our minds to it. This is what I'm planning to do.'

Comfort from outside our group

Sometimes we can feed our negativity to gain reassurance from someone close to us who is not involved in taking the exams. This person can spend a lot of time and energy encouraging and supporting us and helping us to feel more positive.

Subconsciously, we like this, and we can feed off this encouragement and support. But, ask yourself, are you actually listening to the advice, or are you setting up a cycle for yourself where you just want the support? Perhaps the conversation goes something like this:

> 'Mum, I'm going to fail this exam.'
>
> 'Don't be silly dear, of course you won't.'
>
> 'It's really hard, I know I'll fail.'
>
> 'No you won't, you're good at things like this.'
>
> 'No, you don't know just how hard this is for me.'
>
> 'Oh, I'm sure you can do it, here have some cake.'

The underlying message here is something deeper than actually wanting to talk about how to pass the exam. This is an attempt to get praise and support in a general sense; here, our student is convincing themselves that they are going to fail in order to get the message through to their mother that they need support in their life. However, by getting the support, the student is no closer to passing the exam. They are only closer to realising that they are supported by their mother.

This type of interaction is not going to pass your exam for you. What's important to realise is that you can get the same if not better support from those around you by taking the positive approach yourself anyway. Try this:

'Mum, I'm going to pass this exam.'

'Well of course you will, I know that.'

'It's going to be tough but I know I can do it.'

'Yes, I know that too, you're good at things like this.'

'Do you think so? That's great.'

'Oh, I know so. Shall we have some cake?'

When someone is giving you support and encouragement, hear those supportive and encouraging words and remember them when you need a mental boost.

We often learn to think negatively as children so that we do not appear big headed or vain.

Listening to support and encouragement from others is a first step towards feeling supported and encouraged by ourselves throughout our lives.

Today, notice every time someone pays you a compliment, says thank you to you or even smiles at you. Notice it and give yourself a moment to take it in. Don't push the compliment away, as in:

'You're looking great in that outfit.'

'Oh, this old thing, it's nothing.'

Instead, pause, hear the compliment and thank them for it.

What has this got to do with passing your exams? You have been getting encouragement in passing your exams too, so allow yourself to hear it. Take it in and listen to it and give yourself an easier time. Here's a starting point for you from me:

Well done. You've taken such strong positive steps to pass your exam well. You've really made a great move by working through this book and thinking about things in a different way. I know that you're going to do well because you are planning and preparing so well and it's all getting so much easier. You're doing so well, very well done.

When negativity is coming from others

Sometimes we find ourselves in the difficult position of bearing the brunt of someone else's negativity. This might be a parent, a sibling, a boss, teacher or colleague. They somehow don't want us to do well. Is someone giving you subtle messages, perhaps in a joking way, or worse, along the lines of:

> 'You'll never pass, you can't do anything.'
>
> 'He's not cut out for this type of stuff you know.'
>
> 'You'll probably scrape through. It's your brother who's the brainy one.'

Whoever is doing this is not in your shoes. They are not living your life, they are living theirs. They can only imagine how you feel through their own eyes. You are taking this exam, not them. You are taking this exam for your own reasons. Often this kind of criticism is born from insecurity. Not yours, but theirs. They feel the need, for various reasons, to put you down to make themselves feel better.

The best strategy to take with this is to push it aside and to quietly reinforce your own internal positive support. Remind yourself:

'Actually I can do this.'

'I can do this because I have decided to do it.'

'It is my decision, not anyone else's.'

'I am doing this well already.'

The scripts in this book will reinforce your confidence and focus a great deal, so push other people's own issues aside – you don't have time to deal with this, you have exams to pass.

Give yourself some strong positive affirmations

Positive affirmations feel very different to negative statements. Positive affirmations make you feel good and increase your confidence. Increased confidence makes you do things better. Make yourself a nice long list of positive affirmations, both general and specific to passing your exams. Here are some to help you:

'I can and I will pass my exams.'

'I am good at studying and taking exams.'

'I know my subject well, of course I will pass.'

'I already know I am passing my exams.'

'Next year I'll be at university.'

'Everything is going so well now.'

'I'm enjoying my studying now.'

'I'm amazed at how much I know.'

Here is the type of statement to keep off your list:

'I could pass if I worked really hard now.'

'My tutor says I could pass.'

'I'm feeling confident enough to try and do well.'

Don't complicate them by adding conditions, like in the first statement, pushing them away to be someone else's statement, as in the second, or pushing them into the future, as in the third. You are good at passing exams now, and you know it.

The word 'try' weakens your intention. If you have this word in any of your affirmations, take it out.

'I'll try to do as well as I can.'

'I'll try to pass the exam with distinction.'

'I'll try to revise each day.'

Take out the word 'try' and these statements become:

'I'll do as well as I can.'

'I'll pass the exam with distinction.'

'I'll revise each day.'

Now these affirmations are the statements of a candidate who is going to pass the exam and do well. Affirmations lead to positive thought processes which in turn lead to success. An international golfer doesn't go into a tournament with the intention of trying to win the match. They step onto the course knowing that they will win.

Pick out three or four of your most powerful affirmations and use them regularly. Write them down somewhere where you can see them and repeat them often. Say them out loud when you are alone and then repeat them a few times. As you say them, really hear them and let the words sink in. What you tell yourself regularly becomes a reality. By banishing negative statements and using your affirmations often, you set up a positive cycle of confidence, preparation and success for yourself. Then, everything feels and becomes so much easier.

Chapter 10

Other confidence and calmness-building methods

In this chapter, you will be learning tools and methods that you can use on the day of your exam. Take time to set up and practise these methods. Knowing that you have these tools with you in the exam will enhance your confidence and your level of relaxation on the day.

Breathing calm

TIP

Regulating your breathing will regulate other bodily processes, like your heart rate and your blood pressure.

This method is a simple relaxation tool that many of us use all the time anyway, either consciously or not. Although it's simple, I advise that if you have a history of breathing problems, then chat to your doctor before practising any breathing exercises.

Our breathing changes depending on whether we are calm or anxious; and our breathing is something that we can consciously control even though it is usually under our subconscious control.

When we are anxious we have a tendency to over-breathe. This means that we take in too much oxygen, either by breathing too fast or by taking big breaths in. Reversing this consciously means we can breathe ourselves calm.

Exercise

Anxiety is the polar opposite to relaxation. By simply breathing slower and breathing out for longer, we can help ourselves relax.

Take a short breath in and then release it in a nice long sigh, breathing in through your nose and out through your mouth, letting the air whoosh through your teeth and lips. Do this a few times and you will feel more relaxed.

Now enhance the relaxing effect by setting yourself a word that you say through your mind when you breathe out. I suggest a word like 'calm'.

Try this now. Take a gentle breath in, and then breathe out for longer through your mouth and at the same time say the word 'calm' through your mind.

As you do this, you are calming yourself by regulating the amount of oxygen in your body and allowing those overactive physical processes a chance to relax.

Before or during your exam you can take a few moments to do this exercise to promote your feeling of calm.

Anchor

Here is a very useful exercise that you can prepare in advance. You can use it while taking your exam and it works at a subconscious level so you do not need to think about it once you have set it up.

Anchors are based on principles in behavioural psychology and are often used by practitioners of neurolinguistic programming (NLP), a particular branch of hypnotherapy which will be very helpful when you take your exam.

Read this section carefully, and take the time to set up a nice strong anchor for yourself. Once set, you will strengthen it without even thinking about it each time you revise or study, so that it will automatically be in place when you take your exam.

The anchor is so called because you anchor a positive feeling with something else – in this case, an action and a word. Then, each time you use the action and the word, the feeling happens automatically.

TIP

Many professional sportspeople, actors, presenters and speakers use anchors. Set your anchor well and it will serve you whenever you need it.

Exercise

Sit comfortably and relax for a few moments. Concentrate on feelings of lucidity, confidence, calm and control. To help yourself, remember a time when you felt these feelings and remind yourself how they felt at the time. So, sit and remember a time, perhaps in class, when you completely understood everything that was being discussed, you could recall everything that you knew about the subject and you were thinking quickly and clearly. Now, take yourself back to this feeling. This is how it feels to be lucid.

Now, do the same short exercise for those feelings of confidence, calm and control, one at a time. Feeling good now? Excellent.

Now, follow this procedure carefully:

a) Put all the feelings together so you are experiencing lucidity, calm, confidence and control. Allow a word to come into your mind that signifies or describes this compounded feeling for you. Make it a positive word. Here are some examples that my clients have given:

Calm – perfectly describes the state of calm.
Blue – blue reminds me of the beach in Greece where I felt so relaxed and confident.
Jack – name of a small dog that is always so happy.

You only need one word to link with this good positive feeling.

b) Now you need an action. A nice, easy, private action that does not interfere with what you are doing at the time.

As this anchor is for your exams, I suggest an action like picking up your pen. After all, you might be holding your pen or pencil for most of the exam. If your exam involves a different procedure then you can use something different such as pressing your thumb and middle finger together for a few moments. You can do this as often as you want throughout the exam.

c) Now you are going to link those nice, positive feelings with your special word and your special action.

Staying relaxed, focus on feeling lucid, calm, confident and in control. Really experience these feelings, enhancing them as powerfully as you can.

Use whatever resources you need to do this. Imagine that you are breathing the feelings in, or think of a time when you felt the same way; perhaps the time that you scored a goal for your team or received praise from someone you admire, or maybe when you were discussing a subject that you are very interested in or a real expert in.

Really concentrate on these feelings, so that you feel them all over your body, until they are as strong as they can be.

d) As soon as you reach this point of maximum strength, you can set your anchor. You do this by simultaneously saying your special word through your mind and carrying out your special action.

Do this now, enhance the feelings to maximum strength, and at that point say the word over in your mind and perform your special action. Hold it for a few seconds and then relax.

e) Repeat parts c) and d) five or six times. This is vital to set the anchor.

Allow yourself to relax. What you have done is to set up a very powerful association between those feelings, actions and thoughts. The more you use your anchor, the stronger it will become.

For you, the true value of the anchor is that it works the other way around. Want to immediately feel lucid, calm, confident and in control? Simply perform your special action and say your special word in your mind. The feelings will happen automatically.

When you are studying in school or college, or taking mock exams and tests, get into the habit of using your anchor. Each time you do this, your anchor will become stronger.

Your anchor is now a tool that you have with you in your exam. Use it before you start, and use it during your exam any time you need extra feelings of lucidity, confidence, calm and focus.

Regaining control

So everything is going fine in your exam and then you come across something that casts doubt in your mind. Perhaps there is a question that you don't know the answer to, or you realise that you have misinterpreted an instruction and wasted a bit of time. What are you going to do? You are going to put this doubt out of your mind and take positive action. You know that you can gain marks in exams in many ways, and it is usually the case that partly answering a question correctly is much better than not answering it at all.

If you recognise that you have got a little confused or that you don't know something, you are going to dismiss any negative or anxious thoughts and carry on along the positive path that you are taking. There are various practical ways of doing this that you can discuss with your teacher or tutor before the exam.

What we are concerned with here is getting back your concentration and confidence in that moment and realising you can carry on with the remainder of the exam and do your very best. Here is an exercise for letting go of a mistake using visual imagery:

Exercise

Imagine for a moment that you have a little box with a lid in front of you. The box, empty at the moment, is very pretty and beautifully decorated. Take time to imagine this little box, notice its shape and colour, what it's made of, and feel its weight in your hand for a moment. Get to know this little box, it will be of great help to you. Spend a little time familiarising yourself with this box. When you are taking your exam, if you feel at any time that you have made a mistake and those anxiety levels rise, just take a few deep breaths and bring the image of this box into your mind. Then, imagine that you lift the lid from the box, and place the mistake inside. As you do so, your levels of calm and focus grow stronger. Put the lid back on the box. As you do so, your levels of positivity and confidence grow stronger. Place that little box behind you in a safe place. As you do so, you are ready to move on to answer the next question. Later, if you wish, you can re-examine the contents of that box, in an entirely different and more positive way.

Practise these exercises until they are perfect for you. You may not even need to use them in your exam, but knowing that you have these tools will increase your feeling of being in control, and being calm, focused and confident.

Chapter 11

Putting it all together

Well done for reaching the final chapter of this book. By using the exercises and scripts in this book you will now be feeling calm and confident and much more positive about your exam. You have a clearer understanding of how your mind is working and how you will be able to recall all the information you need for the exam. You have planned well, prepared well and you have been taking good care of yourself. You have been promoting your own internal feeling of calm and relaxation, and have set your anchor and created your visualisations. You are now ready to pass that exam confidently and well.

The day of the exam

Having given yourself plenty of time and had a nice early night, you wake up and realise that today is the day of your exam. You feel well rested, refreshed and focused. You feel excited because today is the chance for you to prove to yourself how hard you have been working. Soon, you'll be able to praise yourself for all your efforts.

Spend a few moments just relaxing before you start your day. Do your breathing exercise and say the word 'calm' in your mind. Now you are ready. Have a good, nutritious breakfast to start the day, as it is important to feel well nourished. Eat slowly in order to digest your food properly. Make sure that you have had plenty to drink.

TIP

Tea, coffee and cigarettes are all stimulants, which will serve to increase heart rate and might make you feel more anxious, so avoid these if you can.

If you cannot avoid stimulants, then do not go overboard with them and choose decaffeinated drinks if possible. If you are a smoker, you know that cigarettes do not relax you; in fact, they do the opposite. A few moments of breathing exercises will prove more beneficial.

If you have the choice, dress in something that is comfortable and that makes you feel confident. If you wear glasses to read, then remember to take them with you.

Make sure that you have everything you will need with you: exam entry forms, pens, pencils, identification if you need it. Take water, a watch and tissues, and anything else that you are allowed to take. Ensure that you have a container or bag for everything that is acceptable to take into the exam. Take a deep breath and know that you are ready.

Before the exam

If your exam is late morning or afternoon, you may have some spare time beforehand. This is not the time to get involved in something that is going to take up your mental energy. This should be quiet focus time. Cramming for the exam will not help you to feel calm but you can use this time to quietly have one last read through of your notes. Perhaps you have made some revision cards that contain basic points about the topics you are expected to know and this can be a time to sit and quietly read through them. Keep focused at this point. Whatever you are reading or studying should be relevant to the exam that you are taking later. Here are some suggestions of what you can do before the exam:

- ✓ Read through your revision cards
- ✓ Take a quiet walk
- ✓ Do some light exercise at the gym or swimming pool
- ✓ Do your extended breathing exercise and say your positive affirmations
- ✓ Rehearse your anchor

This is not the time to spend with anxious friends or classmates. If your friends are also feeling calm and confident, which of course we hope they are, then all well and good. Feelings have a habit of feeding from each other – waiting outside the exam room with people who are worrying and talking in loud voices about how they know nothing will not help you. Instead, it is much better to wait somewhere close by until it is time to enter the exam room and then calmly walk in.

If you do decide to study, say firmly to yourself, 'I know this subject and everything I am reading now is confirming to me that I know this subject well.'

When you are ready, ensure that you have everything that you need and then make your way to the exam. Feeling calm and focused, you can use your anchor at any time and, of course, you can practise your breathing exercise too.

During the exam

When you are in the exam room, take your time. Don't worry what anyone else is doing – you have no idea whether they are better prepared than you; chances are they are not, so trust your own judgement. Do things at your pace. Exams are carefully worked out so that you have plenty of time to answer the questions well.

Ensure you take time to follow the instructions that you are given and you thoroughly read through the instructions and the questions before you start.

If you have a choice of questions, and if you don't have to start at the beginning of the paper, then read through everything so that you can decide where to start. You are in control of this exam, not the other way around. Answer this exam in the way that works most effectively for you within the options you have.

Take your time and ensure that you have understood the questions. Having selected the first question to answer, read it again to completely grasp what it is asking. Then, when you are ready, make a start. You'll be feeling calm and focused, relaxed and confident, and you will surprise yourself at how easy it is to recall all the information that you have remembered and stored.

After the exam, you'll be feeling great. Relieved, yes, but also happy, confident and perhaps a little tired. The best efforts can be hard work and now is the time to rest. If you have other exams to take, this rest will allow you some time to put the knowledge that you have been recalling back into your memory so you can focus on the next subject. And don't forget to spend some time congratulating and praising yourself for all your hard work and for knowing all that information.

You have almost reached the end of this book. By now you're feeling so much better than when you first looked at the cover of this book, wondering if it could help. Now, you have a greater understanding of your thoughts and feelings and a greater understanding of how much control you really have over them.

Conclusion

The scripts and exercises in this book have enabled you to grow in confidence and feel a greater sense of inner calm. This confidence is turning your exams into a challenge that you are happy to accept and in which you will do well.

The exercises that you have been working on and the preparations that you have been making will have lasting, positive effects on all areas of your life. Have you noticed that you feel more in control generally? Have you noticed that you feel healthier and fitter and more relaxed?

Many of the methods in this book are regularly used by professional presenters, sportspeople, actors and academics any time where an extra degree of confidence and focus is required. You can continue to use these. Take a moment to look into the future now, knowing that you have all the self-awareness and understanding that you need for whatever challenge may lie ahead.

Acknowledgements

My thanks to all my family, friends and colleagues for their support and encouragement in the writing of this book. My heartfelt thanks too to the fantastic team at Summersdale – in particular, Jennifer, Anna, Lucy and Barney – for their enthusiasm, professionalism, creativity and attention to detail.

GET PAST DRIVING TEST NERVES

Lorna Cordwell

ISBN: 978 1 84024 673 5

Paperback £5.99

*'I'll be so nervous on the day,
I won't be able to do anything.'*

Sounds familiar? Turn your negative thoughts into positive affirmations in this no-nonsense guide, as Harley Street therapist Lorna Cordwell steers you to success in your driving test.

Nearly 60 per cent of driving tests taken in the UK are failed. Most learners admit that nerves are the main cause of the mistakes that lead to test failure. For the thousands who find the driving test a frightening and confidence-destroying experience, help is now at hand.

Praise for *Get Past Driving Test Nerves*

'Though the book targets learner drivers, it essentially provides techniques that may well prove invaluable to anyone preparing for a test situation... this book is written using easy to understand language that clearly explains what causes anxiety, and how you can overcome this by using the exercises provided'

ADVANCED DRIVING INSTRUCTOR NEWS

'... negative thoughts can be turned into positive affirmations by using this no-nonsense guide to steer you towards success'

www.motorbar.co.uk